Books for Education

Letter to My Dreams
for Planet Earth

By
Pilar Vélez

PAR AVION
AIR MAIL
CORREO AEREO

To the visionaries that change the world with the greatness of their Dreams!

To all the children, teenagers, and adults
that love nature and respect the lives of animals,
plants, and planet Earth's resources.
Better human beings for a better planet!

Scan this code to practice the vocabulary and receive Canguro The Postman's mail.

Carta a mis sueños™ / © Letter to my dreams, all rights are reserved to **Pilar Vélez**. Published and distributed by **Snow Fountain Press**.

Letter to My Dreams ™

for Planet Earth

PAR AVION
AIR MAIL
CORREO AEREO

First Edition April 2019
Second Edition April 2020
Third Edition April 2022
©2022, Pilar Vélez

Snow Fountain Press
25 SE 2nd. Avenue, Suite 316 Miami, FL 33131

ISBN: 978-0-9981999-6-2

www.pilarvelez.com
www.snowfountainpress.com

Translated by Silvia Rafti
Copy editing and proofreading by Nellie Rivera Rentas
Editorial Design by Alynor Díaz
Illustrated by Alynor Díaz and Mariet Vergara

Online Platform and workshops promoted by Hispanic Heritage Literature Organization / Milibrohispano.org

@cangurothepostman
@snowfountainpress
@pilarvelezzamparelli

2

Letter to My Dreams

Creative reading and writing to inspire children and teenagers, our future leaders

Letter to My Dreams for Planet Earth ™ is the first volume of the **Letter to My Dreams**™ Collection. These books encourage young readers to protect the environment by learning the life stories of our dreamers. A group of people who have helped safeguard life on our planet and can guide us into the future through their vision, effort, and leadership.

Aware of the significant challenges faced by today's children and teenagers, we want to emphasize the importance of learning more and getting acquainted with the **17 goals of the 2030 Agenda for Sustainable Development adopted by the United Nations**. In this volume, we focused our efforts on those goals designed to protect life in the seas, life on the ground, climate action, and responsible production and consumption.

In this edition, these dreamers share critical aspects of their lives, dreams, and challenges they have overcome or are still battling against to protect the planet and its resources. Their stories show us the need to conquer our fears and dream big, always thinking about the well-being of every life on this earth. It also allows us to recognize that there are many opportunities for those who wish to follow a professional career in science, research, and environmental conservation. Through their stories, our dreamers teach us that **sustainable development** is a mission for all of us. They let us know that each person can lead and inspire others through their values and actions. The planet needs us to make wise and appropriate decisions to face the challenges of our present and those that await us in the future. Each day we fail to provide solutions

is a day wasted that only helps problems to become worse and have a more significant impact. Our dreamers' life stories dreamers, their values, and the series of activities proposed are the basis for understanding the essence of these goals and their implications for the future of humankind.

The educational transversality of **Letter to My Dreams**™ connects and articulates meaningful learning, providing the opportunity to integrate the cognitive and formative aspects. The combination of readings and activities strengthens the connection between the environment's social, cultural, and ethical contexts, thus providing a comprehensive concept of knowledge for their lives. The universal quality of *Letter to My Dreams for the Planet Earth* unites us with no care for race, age, gender, economic status, religion, or beliefs. WE ARE THE EARTH; WE ARE THE LIFE.

Letter to My Dreams complies with the educational and didactic requirements for language learning, enhancing vocabulary, improving reading abilities, oral and written communication. It also encourages creativity and critical thinking. It also positively impacts self-esteem, respect for human rights, and personal empowerment. This volume aims to sensitize readers about the need and urgency to know the environmental challenges we face and to develop responsible attitudes and behaviors about life and the conservation of our planet.

Preserving the LIFE OF THE PLANET is a mission
for the present to ensure the future.

Pilar Vélez

Let's have fun together!
Today is the most important day of our lives.

#55

ACTIVITIES

Pedagogical fundamentals of Letter to My Dreams for the Children of the World

Comprehensive education	Cross-sectional education	Topics
• Education in population • Moral and civic education • Education for peace • Education for gender equality • Environmental education	• Language • Environmental science • Mathematics • Social studies • Artistic education	• Procedural • Conceptual • Attitudinal

Visit our web page: **www.lettertomydreams.com** and practice the vocabulary from the magical trunks on our bilingual English/Spanish platform.

THE WORLD HAS A MASTER PLAN

HELLO! I'M CANGURO THE POSTMAN, FOR THE LETTERS TO MY DREAMS

Making my way with my big "jump, jump," I can reach the many places where the dreamers that write letters to their dreams live. I prefer to hang out in arid zones like steppes and savannahs, dry forests, and prairie lands in New Guinea, Australia, and Tanzania. But I have grown accustomed to jumping between the poles, jungles, mountains, and grasslands searching for the small villages and cities where DREAMERS live. That's where I pick up the letters they write to their dreams.

Through my travels, I have witnessed how our planet changes every day. I've seen many species of flora and fauna threatened, the life of humans too. Just like my Canguro family needs plants, leaves, vegetables, and roots –some of our favorites foods- to eat; other species also need food and a healthy habitat to live. Adequate climate characteristics are required to enjoy this **condition of sustainability**. These include food and water sources and proper soil and air quality for each species. Thus, in a way, all living creatures on this planet share the same needs and resources. But only human beings, with their rationality, sensitivity, and spirit or will, are the only ones capable of positively or negatively impacting their environment. That is why we need people to understand that resources are fragile and limited. They are responsible for not altering or endangering the life of other species, and as a result, of humanity itself. Each of Nature's five kingdoms has its own needs. To ensure their survival, each person must be aware of the positive or negative impact their actions have on the lives of the other species that live on the planet. **That's why I've taken the mission to share with you the powerful message of *Letter to My Dreams for Planet Earth* and tell you what sustainable development is all about.**

6

You are probably asking yourself:

IF THAT IS SO IMPORTANT, WHY DOES NOBODY TALK ABOUT IT?

You would be surprised by the answer: 193 countries, members of the most powerful organization in the world, the United Nations (UN), accepted the challenge to work in what is known as the **2030 Agenda, A MASTER PLAN, containing 17 Sustainable Development Goals (SDGs), the most promising plan for the future of humankind.**

Learn more about the 17 goals for sustainable development and build your dreams! Don't leave any living creature behind!

Welcome aboard to
Letter to My Dreams for Planet Earth

You need to feel that you are part of the planet and that the Earth is part of you.

You and I have a very important mission: PROTECT THE PLANET, ITS SPECIES, AND ITS RESOURCES.

To make it happen, you must open your mind and your heart.

Learn about its problems and how to find solutions. We can't wait for others to do what we can do ourselves now!

Be mindful that Planet Earth has the right to live.

Be optimistic and help inspire others.

Allow yourself to dream and fight for the things you want.

You can help the planet if there's a will to do so.

I believe in you.

I am your dream

ACTIVITIES

#1 I invite you to think about:
Think carefully about the following questions and write down your answers.

What does it mean to respect other people's dreams?

....
....
....

I think dreaming is

....
....
....
....

What does it mean to dream big?

....
....
....

How do you feel when you think about your dream?

....
....
....
....

Only _____ have the power to achieve _____ goals and make _____ dreams come true!

To fulfill my dreams, I need to:

....
....
....
....

#2 Go for a walk!

> Each person has a special dream.

Observe nature and people.
Look at the streets, houses, and trees.
Greet people.
Listen to the sounds and recognize
the universe that surrounds you.
Take a deep breath and value
this moment as a real treasure.
Acknowledge your presence:
you are a unique, wonderful being who lives
on a planet you must protect.

I'm SPECIAL

Every person is unique and valuable
Find out just how wonderful you are!

#3 Paint inclusion and diversity. Use the whole color palette. Express yourself!

My Planet and I

Hello,

I am your dream. I invite you to explore our planet Earth: where you and I live, and where we will have the best of times.

In each star, draw an important part of your life, what you love, and the things you need to live.

Which one of these stars do you need to live?

Color them or mark them with just one color.

Write them on a list and explain why each is important to you.

• What happens if one of these stars fades out? **Cover one of them with your hand. Think about what would happen and how it would affect you.**

Earth also wants to join in. It wants you to write in each star the name of a living being or inanimate thing that you know.

Cover one star with your hand.

- What happens if one of these stars fades out?
- How are the other stars affected?

Our planet only has one life, and each part fulfills a vital function.

There is nothing left to fate on the planet. There is a **fundamental principle** of balance that holds the chain of life together. Order, processes, elements, and relations must be maintained to sustain what exists today. If any changes affect it negatively, it will threaten the lives of other species and, ultimately, our own existence.

Did you know that the Earth is 4,543 billion years old and that it changes every second?

"Opening the meeting, our elected President, the Giant armadillo of South America."

"And where is the Executive Secretary, the Polar bear?"

"He wasn't able to come, Mr. Armadillo. The Arctic fox notified us that the melting of the ice trapped the Polar bear. Let's do a roll call," said the bee while buzzing around the participants.

"Javan rhinoceros?   present

"Amazon tiger?"   present

"Kangaroo?"

"He has not arrived," exclaimed the giraffe while stretching her neck.

"Bluefin tuna?"   present

"Mountain gorilla?"   present

"Is Penguin present?"   present

"Monarch butterfly?"   present

"Leatherback sea turtle?"   present

"Iberian lynx?"   present

"Sloth? And don't laugh..."   p r e s e n t

"Black-footed ferret?"   present

"California condor?"   present

"Sumatran orangutan?"   present

"Bactrian camel?"   present

"Blue whale?"   present

"Dolphin?"   present

"Seal?"   present

"Panda bear?"   present

"Sea corals?"   present

"And where are the rest?" asked Mr. Armadillo, alarmed.   present

"We couldn't locate them," answered the bee. "We sent the Andean condor, but he hasn't returned. Then we sent the Chilean woodstar, but the area where he lives was fumigated, and we have received no news. Later, we sent the Burrowing parrot, but he was on his way there when some bird traffickers caught him and put him in a big cage."

"And why isn't the European mink here? Did anyone inform him about our emergency assembly?"

"We tried, Mr. Armadillo. We sent a message with the Mediterranean monk seal, who warned us that they are still being hunted and that an invading species is threatening their region. In any case, we are still looking for them with some contacts of our friend, the Giant lizard of El Hierro."

"And where's the Giant lizard of El Hierro?"

"He hasn't come either, sir," answered the bee while coughing and sneezing. It continued, "As you see, honorable colleagues of the assembly, the situation is critical. An inmmediate solution is urgently needed; otherwise, none of us will reach the next meeting. There are many cases where the number of animals of a species is down to just a few hundred specimens. And in other cases, we don't know if they have become extinct."

"I suggest we hold a worldwide protest," said the Harpy eagle. "Let's go to the cities together and demand our rights. We have rights, don't we?"

"That would be suicide," replied the Spectacled bear while moving his head from side to side. "They will massacre us. Cities are not a place for us."

"But we don't have a voice!" exclaimed the Beluga whale, worried. "I don't think we have the power to do anything. We can't clean plastic from the oceans, stop global warming, or the use of pesticides, or prevent trees from being chopped down. Or the illegal trafficking of animals, the entry of invasive species, overfishing, or the pollution and contamination that poisons soil, water, and air."

"The seas are becoming uninhabitable," said the Wood turtle. "Thousands of our brothers drown as a consequence of the oil spills and the waste thrown into the sea."

"The melting ice is starving us to death, and we are disappearing little by little," said the Polar bear, who managed to reach the assembly.

"So many trees have been cut down that we don't have anywhere to fly onto, or where to make our nests anymore," added the Toucan.

"What Mr. Toucan says is true. There are hardly any gardens with flowers or prairies left and, in their place, there are ranches and roads. What is going on? There is so much poison that I don't believe we will be able to survive." This came from the Karner blue butterfly, which spread its wings while being surrounded and hugged by its colleagues.

"There must be a solution," replied the owl. "We have to survive. We can't afford to die. Wouldn't it be a sad world without us on the planet? I can't imagine the rainforest without the tiger, or the jungle without its Amazon River dolphin, or the sea without sharks. Each one of us deserves to live."

They were all inconsolable when, suddenly, the kangaroo arrived, reaching the attendees with his long hops. He looked happy. The smile on his face looked like a half-moon.

"The kangaroo has arrived!" all shouted when they saw him.

"Why do you look so happy? None of us can do anything and we're going to die!" said the Mexican sheartail, crying.

"Perhaps we don't have the solution, but I know who has it!" exclaimed the kangaroo loudly. "I have traveled around the world, and there are millions of people fighting for us. We must hold on!"

The animals jumped for joy along with the kangaroo, and they hugged him. At the same time, he took from his bag thousands of letters written by the **visionaries that transform the world thanks to the greatness of their dreams.**

"If they believe they can do it, I believe it too," stated the kangaroo, clasping a bunch of letters to his heart.

Have you sent your letter already?
Your dreams are needed and they make a difference!

16

ACTIVITY

#6 Read the General Assembly of the United Endangered Species (GAUES) fable. In your opinion, which goals of the 2030 Agenda help protect species and their habitats?

_____
Goal: _____
Because: _____
_____
_____

_____
Goal: _____
Because: _____
_____
_____
_____

_____
Goal: _____
Because: _____
_____
_____
_____

_____
Goal: _____
Because: _____
_____
_____

_____
Goal: _____
Because: _____
_____
_____
_____

_____
Goal: _____
Because: _____
_____
_____

_____
Goal: _____
Because: _____
_____
_____

Chest of Words from the
GENERAL ASSEMBLY OF THE UNITED ENDANGERED SPECIES (GAUES)

Trafficker

Melting

Pollutants

Global Warming

Invasive Species

Fungicides

Waste **FELLING**

Hunting

Extinction

Pollution

Deforestation

Overfishing

Melting

From the chest of words from the Assembly of the United Endangered Species (AUES), select the term that best suits each definition on the following list:

- _____: a person dedicated to illegally (not lawful) market merchandise or products prohibited under the law—for example, animal trafficker.

- _____: increase in the temperature of Earth's oceans and atmosphere associated in part to the emissions of greenhouse gases due to human activities, such as burning fossil fuels and changes in the use of lands, as in deforestation.

- _____: strip a piece of land from all forest plants. The action and effect of deforesting.

- _____: are substances used to eliminate or prevent the growth of fungi or molds that are harmful to plants or animals. Fungicides are classified according to the way they act, composition, and field of application.

- _____: plants or animals introduced to ecosystems different from their own, thus becoming plagues. By adapting and colonizing their new ecosystems, they alter and overpopulate them since they have no natural predators to control their growth or extinguish them.

- _____: trash, residues.

- _____: refers to the action to cut down vast amounts of trees, eliminating forests.

- _____: refers to removing forests and plants in a specific place, generally by felling or burning.

- _____: the action to pursue an animal to catch and kill it.

- _____: the disappearance of a species of animal or plant.

- _____: a natural process due to the change of season when temperatures start to rise, melting snow and ice. The melting process has accelerated due to the hole in the ozone layer on Earth's atmosphere, which causes the greenhouse effect and the resulting global Warming.

- _____: the excessive fishing of fish and shellfish with devastating effects for ecosystems.

- _____: in Ecology refers to a specific type of contamination characterized as intense and harmful and present in the air and water. It is the result of industrial and biological waste.

- _____: physical or chemical agents that can harmfully alter the original or normal condition of an environment.

Here are some members of the General Assembly of United Endangered Species (GAUES). Study the following list and write the name of the corresponding animal under its photo/image.

1. Axolotl
2. Andean condor
3. Chilean Woodstar
4. European mink
5. Mountain gorilla

6. Iberian lynx
7. Olm
8. Sumatra tiger
9. White rhinoceros
10. Snow leopard

11. Panda bear
12. Chimpanzee
13. Tapir
14. Mandrill
15. Mediterranean monk seal

16. Simony's lizard Gallotia simonyi
17. Lemurs
18. Manis
19. Saiga antelope
20. Red-crowned crane

ACTIVITY

#9 Even though it may seem impossible, we can help endangered species in many ways. Below, you will find four ways we can do so. Fill in the missing ways, and most importantly, adopt an environmentally friendly lifestyle. Our Planet will appreciate it.

1. **Reduce our carbon footprint.** Be sure to disconnect electronics that are not in use at the moment. Making smart use of electricity and appliances such as clothes washers and dryers also helps.

2. **Make donations, become a volunteer or join** an environmental or conservationist organization.

3. **Don't purchase furniture made from illegally cut forest trees.**

4. **Use less plastic.** Mainly try to avoid purchasing bottles or drinks packaged in plastic containers.

5. ....

6. ....
....
....
....

7. ....
....
....
....

8. ....
....
....

9. ....
....
....

Did you know that only an estimated 2,000 giant pandas live in their natural habitat and they are all in China's tempered forests?

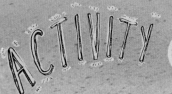 **ACTIVITY**

#10 Becoming aware of their existence is the first step in helping.

1. Choose Sone of the animals mentioned in the (GAEAU) and research all you can about it.

   Answer the following questions:

   a. Where does it lives, and what does it eat?

   b. Can you describe its physical appearance?

   c. What threats does it face?

   d. How many individuals of its species are left today?

   e. Are there any organizations or projects aimed at protecting it from extinction?

   f. How can you help?

2. Prepare a presentation with photos or drawings and share it with your parents, friends, and teachers.

ACTIVITY

#11 Based on the story, identify 5 sustainable goals that would help animals survive.

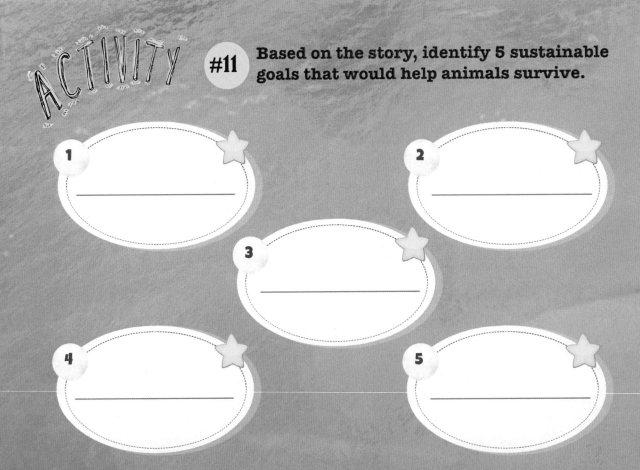

1 _____

2 _____

3 _____

4 _____

5 _____

#12 RESIDUES, FUNGICIDES, AND POLLUTANTS

Assemble your classmates and join together to recognize the difference between these three words.
Research and debate the following:

1 What effects do residues, fungicides, and pollutants have on our planet?

2 Do we need fungicides to live? Draw a table about the pros and cons of using fungicides.

3 What impact do residues and the use of fungicides have on climate change?

4 What would happen if humanity failed to control the amount of residues and pollutants and the use of fungicides?

5 Suggest at least five actions that could help to improve the quality of the air we breathe and reduce the impact of residues, fungicides, and pollutants.

Always remember that your ideas are valuable and needed to find solutions!

IT'S TIME TO BREAK GROUND!

• Think about all the waste found around you and find a way to use them to create a product that can be used to satisfy a need.

I AM MY PLANET TOO

With this activity, we will try to see the planet within ourselves. In the same way, we are a part of it, and it is also part of us.

*For this activity, you will need the largest sheet of paper you can find. FOLLOW THESE INSTRUCTIONS STEP BY STEP.

Step # 1 Lay down, on your back, on top of the sheet of paper, with your arms extended. Ask a friend or relative to trace your silhouette.

Step # 2 Make and color a drawing of planet Earth inside your silhouette.

Include the following:

- The continents, seas, mountain ranges, valleys, volcanoes, mountain peaks, lakes, and rivers.
- The vegetation: rainforests, forests, mangroves, and brushwoods.
- The animals: mammals, fish, birds, reptiles, and amphibians
- The map of your country.
- Mark the location of your city.
- Your home, school, a park, and other places you frequently visit.

Draw and color the planet's surroundings

Step # 3 Now imagine that you are planet Earth.

1 How do you feel being part of the universe?

2 What makes you unique within the universe?

3 What do you like the most about being planet Earth?

4 What do you feel when the trees in your mountains are cut down?

5 What do you think about those who pollute your waters?

6 What do you feel when your animal and plant species are exterminated and your forest disappear?

7 What happens when trash, plastic, and chemicals are thrown into your rivers and seas?

Step # 4 Write messages to the different parts of planet Earth that you drew inside of your silhouette.

Step # 5 Write a thank you list to all those elements of nature that allow you to live and enjoy life.

Think about

- When you colored the planet, which colors did you use the most? Why?
- What do these colors symbolize?
- Did you feel the planet as a part of you?
- If the Earth is a part of you, as you are of it, what can you do to take care of it?

Imagine

Today, planet Earth has 194 countries, 1,961,969 cities, and it's inhabited by 7.53 billion people, according to the 2017 census. Before we populated the planet like this:

- What was on it? What has been lost?
- What changes have occurred, and how have they affected the planet?
- Which of the current changes can you control?
- How does your perception of the planet change if you see it as a part of you?
- How would you teach other people to see the planet as part of themselves and feel it as their own?

* You can modify this written exercise by lying down, face-up, with your arms spread out on a flat surface. Ask a friend or relative to trace the shape of your body on the floor with chalk. You will need coloring chalks and objects to help you better represent what you want to express.

USE YOUR CREATIVITY!

CLIMATE CHANGE is Our Greatest Challenge

Have you ever wondered...

What was the weather like a century ago?
How was the climate in your city 30 years ago?
How was the climate in your city 90 years ago?
How will the climate be in the future?

How's the weather today?

Is it raining?

Is it hot?

Is it cloudy?

Is it humid?

Is it cold?

You probably haven't asked yourself any of these questions, except those that seem everyday happenstance. Nonetheless, it's not just about taking out the umbrella when it's raining outside or wearing a hat in summer and remembering to put on sunscreen to protect our skin against the sun's ultraviolet rays. **Climate is a crucial condition for our survival. We must be aware that it is changing and that there are urgent actions that we must learn about and embrace!**

Climate is a natural phenomenon. It results from the variation in patterns of different elements, including temperature, atmospheric pressure, humidity, wind, precipitation, and other meteorological conditions. These characterize the climate in a specific geographical region and, thus, the type of vegetation and the main fauna found in each place.

Did you know that to determine the climate in each region and learn if it has changed, climatologists analyze recorded daily values of each of these elements every 30 years to develop an average climate condition for each area?

The latest studies have shown that Earth's climate has changed at an unprecedented speed since the pre-industrial era, before the period between 1750 and 1800. Since the Industrial Revolution, it is estimated that the planet's temperature has increased by nearly 1.2 grades Celsius (1.2 °C, equivalent to 2.16 °F). Said increase has taken place during a century, a relatively short time considering that climate changes usually take millions of years to happen. This phenomenon has been identified as **climate change**, and global warming (GW) results from this process. Scientists worldwide agree that carbon dioxide emissions (CO2) due to the burning of fossil fuels, such as carbon, oil, and natural gas to produce energy, are the cause of this phenomenon.

The Turn Down the Heat report prepared for the World Bank by the Potsdam Institute for Climate Impact Research (PIK) and Climate Analytics warns us about the urgency to act. If the present tendency continues, the Earth's temperature will rise up to 4 degrees Celsius (4 °C, equivalent to 7.2 degrees Fahrenheit 7.2 °F) by 2100. If this happens, it will have grave consequences, including city floods, an increase in malnutrition (hunger), health problems, shortage of food, the disappearance of coral reefs, the rise in sea levels, and unbearable heat waves that will impact the lives of all the species living in the planet, including humans.

The oceans have been fundamental in fighting climate change since they provide half of the oxygen we breath and regulate the planet's weather and temperature. A significant part of the heat that we have added to the Earth due to human activities has been absorbed by the oceans, which in return are being affected by high carbon dioxide emissions.

"...We can, and we must avoid an increase of 4 degrees in the world's temperature; we have to stop the warming of the planet, so it won't surpass 2 degrees... If we fail to adopt measures regarding climate change, we face the risk of leaving to our children a world that will be completely different from the world we live in today..."

Jim Yong Kim
doctor, anthropologist, and former president of the World Bank
Source: https://www.bancomundial.org/

We can no longer change the past,
but we can transform the future with our actions in the present!

#14 **Analyze and write in your workbook...**

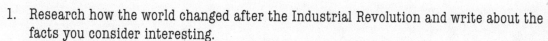

1. Research how the world changed after the Industrial Revolution and write about the facts you consider interesting.
2. Explain in your own words what is the greenhouse effect, global warming, and their consequences.
3. Why is it essential for us to be aware of this problem?
4. How do you feel now that you understand what is happening with the Earth's climate?
5. Identify which is the sustainable goal regarding climate. How does this goal impact the others included in the master plan?
6. Do you think we would be able to reduce carbon dioxide emissions (CO2)? How?

CLIMATE CHANGE

Climate change affects the basic needs of human beings and animal species, including their habitats.

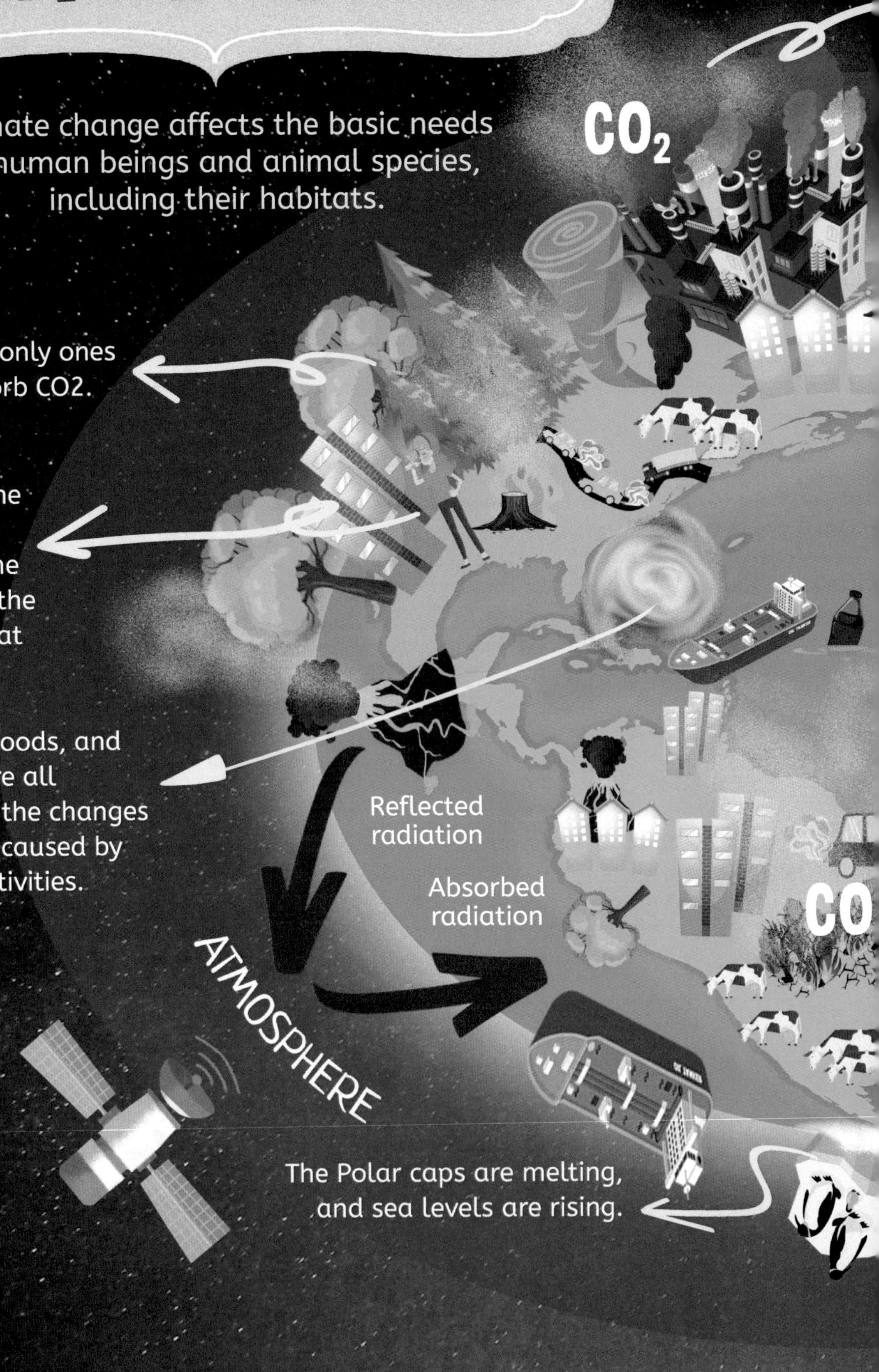

CO_2

Trees are the only ones that can absorb CO2.

The greater the concentration of GEG is in the atmosphere, the higher the heat retention.

Hurricanes, floods, and heatwaves are all connected to the changes in the Planet caused by mankind's activities.

Reflected radiation

Absorbed radiation

CO

ATMOSPHERE

The Polar caps are melting, and sea levels are rising.

The use of fossil fuels (coal, oil, natural gas) created the emissions that have caused the greenhouse effect gases (GEG).

SOLAR RADIATION

Greenhouse effect gases (GEG) cause the accumulation of infrared radiation and high temperatures in the atmosphere. Industries and cattle raising generate GEG, which causes global warming.

CO2

CO_2

When urban waste is burned, a significant amount of pollutants are emitted into the atmosphere.

It is estimated that global warming will increase the temperature to 16.5°C, and scientists are worried that the consequences would be catastrophic if surpassed.

ACTIVITIES

#15   Your actions regarding our climate can make a difference!

a. Now that you know about the problem do some research and determine what you can do towards the solution. The following table presents eleven aspects or recommendations that require our immediate action. Fill in the table, and you'll find out all the things we can do!

Recommendation	Action What can we do? Write your answer.
Water	
Education	
Transportation	
Paper	
Government	
Trees	
Trash	
Energy	
Food	
Chemical Products	
Consumption	
Keep the list going... There's so much more we can do!	

b. Make a presentation about climate change and the solutions you have learned to address it for your classmates. Encourage them to be part of the solution too. **Remember that you are a visionary that transforms the world with the greatness of your dreams. Be optimistic and take that first step!**

Start by doing what's necessary; then do what's possible; and suddenly, you will be doing the impossible.

Saint Francis of Assisi

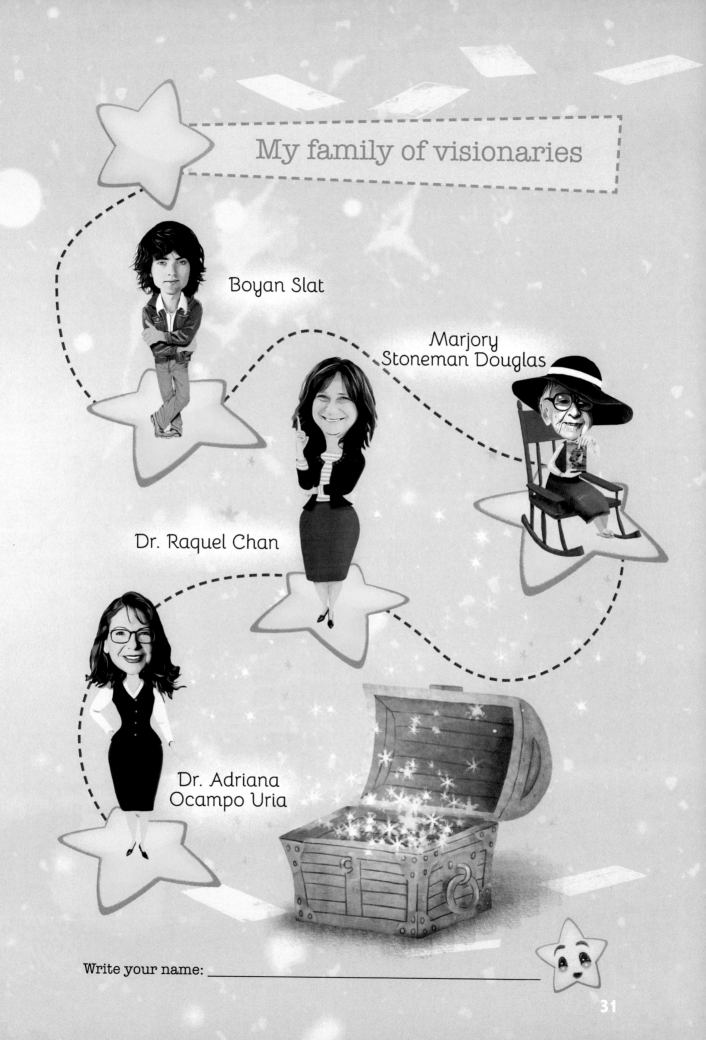

My family of visionaries

Boyan Slat

Marjory
Stoneman Douglas

Dr. Raquel Chan

Dr. Adriana
Ocampo Uria

Write your name: _____

BOYAN SLAT

The Netherlands, 1994

"If you want to do something, do it as soon as possible."

Did you know that plastic is a material that the planet can't digest?

Can you imagine how our oceans would be without garbage or plastic bottles?

A nineteen-year-old boy did. And best of all, he had the initiative and the courage to put his idea into practice. Boyan Slat was born in The Netherlands in 1994, and he invented a system that uses sea currents to collect plastic and clean the oceans. His invention can reduce the cleaning time by many years, something many scientists considered almost impossible, as it was estimated to take at least 79,000 years to achieve.

Boyan's interest in finding a solution to the problem came up while diving in Greece in 2011 when he was sixteen. He was alarmed to discover that instead of fish, he mostly saw plastic waste at the bottom of the sea. Using a thin net that he had made, he noticed that seawater contained not only large objects but also a myriad of tiny plastic particles. He wondered why no one had done anything to solve this problem. Or whether anyone was concerned about what was happening. This experience impacted him so much that he took advantage of the opportunity to work on a school project to do his own research about the topic.

Step by step, until reaching a possible solution...

The first step that Boyan took was understanding how nature works and studying the problem of marine pollution. He learned that plastic gathers up in vast areas due to ocean gyres (marine current system). This knowledge allowed Boyan to design a passive system using wind, waves, and sea currents as the only energy source to catch and collect the plastic garbage that contaminates the oceans.

It is a floating barrier -more than 62 miles long- that collects plastic waste without affecting sea life. Finally, sea currents drag the trash to the center of the structure, where it is compiled into a storage tower. It is then sorted, processed, and transported to land every six weeks. It can then be commercialized, making it a self-sufficient system that generates its own energy source.

Part of the solution to the plastic contamination issue is finding a way to recycle that material. The system designed by Boyan is about 33% cheaper than traditional methods, as the young inventor explained. Before finalizing his model, Boyan and his team had to run many tests with hardly any economic resources. Their desire to make the system work motivated them to overcome all obstacles.

"We went through the Stone Age, the Bronze Age, and now we live in the Plastic Age," said Boyan at a TED Conversation event. He pointed out that many people believe that environmental damage is a problem that will need to be solved by future generations. And as a young person, he was calling out for people not to wait any longer and start solving the problem now that it was possible. His talk had a significant impact, and the video went viral, exceeding two million visits.

Boyan's project received the support of many people. But it also faced criticism from those who questioned if it would work and its environmental impact. Boyan and his team of engineers and scientists are focused on perfecting his design and the strategy to increase its success rate. Another group of scientists has validated the results and considers the project financially viable.

In June 2014, Boyan told the world that within 10 years, it was possible to clean at least half of the big stain of trash in the Pacific Ocean known as *The Great Pacific Garbage Patch*.

Since then, the project has grown. Thanks to a strategy called crowdfunding, which helps to collect donations from any part of the world to finance large projects, Boyan managed to gather enough resources to continue with the stages of development. He used social media to make the project known and raise international awareness about the need to implement it, gaining the support of engineers, volunteers, and scientists worldwide to join The Ocean Cleanup, the organization he founded in 2013. The goal is to clean 90% of the plastic accumulated in the ocean by 2040.

Never before had the scientific community embarked on a project of this magnitude in the ocean. Since its beginnings in 2014, work has been done fixing glitches on the pilot system and investigating the problem of plastic pollution in the oceans.

In 2018, The Cleanup launched the first pilot system (System 001) from San Francisco, California, composed of a 2,000 foot-long floating pipe called Wilson. Its mission was to deal with the largest isle of floating garbage between San Francisco and Hawaii. The system presented some errors and had to be submitted for revision and maintenance, so a new launch is expected in the future.

In the face of the fears that many people and organizations have expressed, Boyan argues: What happens is that what we are doing is something that has never been done before... "It's 100 times bigger than anything that's ever been deployed in the ocean," he said. "It's 50% deeper and 10 times more remote than the world's most remote oil rig. So obviously, there are technical challenges."

Boyan's life revolves around this great goal. His compromise implies great sacrifices in his personal and social life.

He even quit seeking his degree in Aerospace Engineering to devote himself full-time to *The Ocean Cleanup*. Boyan has been recognized as one of the twenty most promising young entrepreneurs in the world (Intel EYE50). He is also the youngest person to have obtained one of the UN's highest environmental recognitions: *Champions of the Earth*. In 2015, King Harald of Norway awarded him the Young Entrepreneur Award for the maritime industry. His name appears in the Global Thinkers 2015 list, the 2016 Forbes edition "30 under 30", and Reader's Digest has named him European of the Year. The Ocean Cleanup was considered one of the Designs of the Year by the London Design Museum and received the 2015 INDEX: Award; it won Fast Company's Innovation by Design Awards.

TIME Magazine also chose it as one of the best twenty-five inventions of 2015.

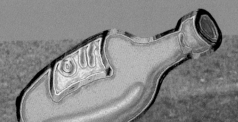

> "Only if we realize that change is more important than money, the money will come."
> **Boyan Slat**

Plastics are made from materials found in nature, like natural gas, oil, coal, minerals, and plants.

Did you know that a rubber, tree produces a milky sap called latex or rubber?

Look for information about rubber, and you will discover some fascinating stories.

Where does the garbage go?

A big part of it is poured into our rivers, reaching the sea.

OYASHIO
BERING
ALASKA
NORTH PACIFIC
KUROSHIO
CALIFORNIA
CONVERGENCE ZONE
NORTH EQUATORIAL
EQUATORIAL COUNTERCURRENT
SOUTH EQUATORIAL

Due to the shortage of materials like ivory or turtle shell, scientists of the XIX century decided to use cellulose. When heated with chemical products, this substance found in plants and trees can become an extremely durable new material: *synthetic plastic.*

Nowadays, the raw materials used to produce plastic come from hydrocarbons easily available in natural gas, oil, and coal.

ACTIVITY

#16 We produce almost 300 million tons of plastic every year, and only 9% gets recycled annually.

Look around you and make a list of all the items made of (or contain) plastic.

There are approximately 150 million tons of plastic in the sea.

Do you think all these items must be made partially or entirely of plastic?

_____

_____

_____

_____

_____

_____

_____

How long does it take for these items to disappear?

Cardboard box
2 MONTHS

Cotton fibers
14 MONTHS

Laminated wood
3 YEARS

Newspapers
6 WEEKS

Fruit peels
7 WEEKS

Milk carton
3 MONTHS

Woolen socks
1-5 YEARS

Plastic containers
100 YEARS

Aluminum
200 YEARS

Cigarettes
1-5 YEARS

Plastic rings
400 YEARS

Foam cups
60 YEARS

Plastic bags
20 YEARS

Plastic bottles
450 YEARS

Disposable diapers
475 YEARS

Nylon threads
600 YEARS

Glass
Not determined

As you can see, garbage does not magically disappear. A big part of it ends on our beaches, carried back and forth by the waves and tides; furthermore, marine animals consume it because they confuse waste with food. Plastic items decompose until being reduced to fragments that pollute all the seas of our planet and affect most ecosystems and, of course, the food chain.

Did you know that approximately 1.4 billion pounds of waste are thrown into the ocean?

- Research some environmental protection organizations.
- Learn about their work.
- Select one of the organizations and write in your notebook the data you found most interesting about it.
- Share that information with your classmates.

VISITA:
https://theoceancleanup.com/
and learn about the biggest cleaning project in history

#18

You have the power to transform the world and to impact the planet's life with yours.

Arrange conversations with your friends and family.
Tell them about Boyan's story and raise these questions:

- Plastic takes hundreds of years to decompose in the environment, and it is known that some types take even a thousand years to do so. Then why are we using such a long-lasting material?

- If plastic is a contaminating material that threatens living beings, why are we still using it, ignoring the damage that it causes?

- Before reading about Boyan Slat's work, did you know that plastic pollutes the planet?

- Do you think it is necessary to inform the community about the use of plastic?

- Can we survive without those articles made of plastic? If so, how?

- Where does the issue lie?

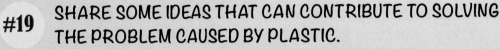

#19 SHARE SOME IDEAS THAT CAN CONTRIBUTE TO SOLVING THE PROBLEM CAUSED BY PLASTIC.

I think that _____
_____
_____
_____

#20   Based on Boyan Slat's story and the problems the environment faces, what life lessons can you draw from this reading?

_____
_____
_____
_____
_____

**"WE ARE NATURE.
Anything we do against it goes
against ourselves."**

Pilar Vélez

#21   Get inspired and write your own sentences:

We are _____
_____
_____

Nature _____
_____
_____
_____

BOYAN SLAT'S
MAGICAL CHEST OF WORDS

Sustainable

Ocean gyre Environmental Impact

Strategy

Feasible Ecology

Understanding

CROWDFUNDING

*"We forget that the **water cycle** and the **life cycle** are one."*

Jacques Y. Cousteau
French naval officer, explorer, and researcher.

#23

Look for the biography and some videos about the life of Jacques Y. Cousteau on the Internet.

Write down in your notebook the answers to the following questions:

· What made him famous?
· What was he passionate about?
· What is his legacy?
· On a sheet of paper, draw the water cycle.

ACTIVITY #24

Using Boyan's Chest of Words, select the word that matches the meaning of each word on the following list:

- _____: consists in making public the need for funds for a cause or project. It is a practice in which a large number of people can give small amounts of money via donations and contributions, made mainly through the Internet, to finance such projects.

- _____: the ability to think. Have a clear idea about a particular subject. Major knowledge about something, knowing, comprehend, infer, deduce, discern.

- _____: a field of study within the biological sciences that studies the relationships between living organisms, including plants and animals, with their biophysical environment. It also includes the interactions that determine the distribution, abundance, number, and organization of organisms living in different ecosystems.

- _____: a plan of action designed by a person or a group to achieve a major or overall objective. "Strategy can be defined as the determination of the long-term goals and objectives of an enterprise, and the adoption of courses of action and the allocation of resources necessary for carrying out these goals." (A. Chandler)

- _____: capable of being done or carried out. It also refers to the availability of resources needed to implement an objective or project successfully.

- _____: any large system of circulating ocean currents, particularly those involved with the Earth's rotation. There are five ocean gyres: the North Atlantic Gyre; the South Atlantic Gyre; the Indian Ocean Gyre; the North Pacific Gyre; and the South Pacific Gyre.

- _____: the effect that human activity have on the environment. Any change to the environment's natural state.

- _____: in Ecology and Economics, it refers to something that can be sustained for an extended period without depleting resources or it's not likely to damage the environment. It also refers to the equilibrium of a species with its ecosystem's resources.

#25 There are several words in Boyan's trunk that are key when planning a project:

1. _____ 2. _____

3. _____ 4. _____

5. _____

Do you know any other words that we could add to this list?

_____

_____

_____

"He who has the will has the power."
Menander of Athens
(342 BC – 292 BC)
Greek playwright.

Like Boyan, each person can develop a plan to find solutions to their needs and their environment. **Do you have the willpower to do it?**

ACTIVITY

#26 Read our dreamer's biography, and in each rhombus, write the number of the corresponding sustainable goal mentioned in their/his/her life story.

In your notebook, write the answers to the following question:
How does the project led by Boyan Slat and his team help achieve these goals?

ACTIVITY

#27 Read carefully and write the answers in your notebook.

Have you ever wondered...
How will you use your talent, knowledge, or energy?

The oldest remains ever found and attributed to the Homo sapiens are 315 000 years old. This number may not seem that old compared to the 4543 billion years of planet Earth. And as you might imagine, over time, many things have changed for the planet and us as a species. We went from making tools out of stone to building pyramids, bridges, transatlantic ships, machines, trains, airplanes, computers, robots, satellites, spaceships, cities, dams, drilling platforms at sea, and nuclear plants. And with the help of science, we have even gone as far as to create new species indirectly. If you look carefully around you, you will notice how human beings can transform and impact nature, both positively and negatively. The world we live in is the result of evolution and our actions.

I FIGTH FOR MY DREAMS

ACTIVITY #28

Have you ever wondered...
How would your life impact
the planet?

LET ME TELL YOU A STORY:

The sea that died of thirst

The Aral Sea was the fourth-largest endorheic lake or inland sea in the world, located in Central Asia, between Uzbekistan and Kazakhstan. Once, it had an area of 67 300 kilometers and was home to at least 100 species of fish and provided food for 200 species of mammals and 500 species of birds that lived in the surrounding dry steppes. Its resources represented the livelihood of thousands of fishers, providing a sixth of all the fish consumed in the Soviet Union.

During the 1960s, the Soviet Union (the former USSR) detoured the water coming from Sir Daria and Amu Daria rivers that ran through some shared areas of the former Soviet republics of Uzbekistan, Kazakhstan, Turkmenistan, Kirgizstan, and Tajikistan. They did this to use the water needed to increase the extension of locations used to grow rice and cotton, which at the time were the most profitable crops. As a result of this action, the Aral Sea didn't receive the water it needed to sustain itself. The climate in the area also changed since rain became less and less frequent and temperatures began to rise. Of the former Aral Sea, all that remains are small lakes. These represent 10 percent of the original lake's area, and their high salinity makes them unsuitable for sustaining life. What used to be an ancient lake of thousands and thousands of years is now a big smear of dried, yellowish land with ships stuck in the sand that can be seen all the way from the satellites in space.

Also, the people living in nearby populations are facing severe health problems. Due to the changes in climate patterns, they now experience continuous sandstorms that carry salt and toxic substances from pesticides and fertilizers, causing severe illnesses amongst its inhabitants.

...And that's how water became salt.

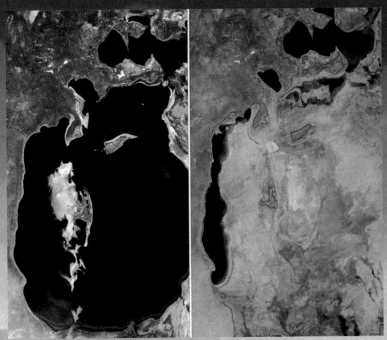

NASA. Public domain photo. September 30, 2014. Comparison of the Aral Sea in 1989 and 2014.

ACTIVITY

#29 DEBATE

Create two groups and assign a stance to each one. The first group will present three reasons to detour rivers' natural courses to develop large crop zones. The second group will give three reasons why they should not do this type of project. After presenting their positions, the two groups must come up with a solution that will facilitate equilibrium and harmony for both parties.

Thinkers' Roundtable ▷ **#30** Gather up your friends and, as a team, find a solution for the next challenge.
Follow the instructions:

- Identify which sustainable goals relate to this story.
- Draw the rain cycle and compare it to the situation experienced at the Aral Sea. Analyze how the disappearance of the lake affects climate patterns.
- Do you think that Boyan Slat's story gives any ideas that, if put into place, could help restore the Aral Sea?
- Research and learn more about the Aral Sea and develop a plan to bring life back to this lake. Think carefully about the resources you'll need. Don't limit your imagination, be creative.
- Present your plan and provide backup for your ideas. Be a visionary dreamer!

"Imagination is more important than knowledge. For knowledge is limited to all we know and understand, while imagination embraces the entire world, and all there ever will be to know and understand."
Albert Einstein

LISTEN TO THE VOICE OF **MARJORY STONEMAN DOUGLAS**

United States, 1890

"We cannot preserve what we do not have".

The "Grandmother of the Glades"

Many men and women have led the battle to preserve the environment in all corners of the planet. Among them, there was Marjory Stoneman Douglas, who was born on April 7th, 1890, in Minneapolis, Minnesota, and passed away on May 14th, 1998, in Coconut Grove, Florida, at the age of 108. She felt a strong inclination for reading and high sensitivity toward nature from a very young age. She graduated with a degree in English from Wellesley College in 1912. Later, in 1915, she traveled to Miami and based her place of residence there until the end of her days.

Many people who met her remember her with admiration and longing. Her name is bound to a precious treasure, the Everglades, and its fragile ecosystem. Her mission was to protect this habitat against the threat of being drained and have the land used for construction developments that would forever change the ecological order of this unique reserve. The battle Marjory undertook to preserve the natural resources in South Florida granted her national and international fame. And her name is among the most renowned environmental activists in the world. She led a campaign that lasted her entire life. Her heart and determination, combined with her passion and mastery of the art of communication and language, were the essential resources to convey the powerful message that impacted all spheres of society. Her **passion**, **leadership**, and writing **creativity** all converged with the marked **objectivity** of a great journalist. Using her typewriter, she wrote reports and stories for the Miami Herald, short stories for adolescents and adults, and multiple letters. She didn't know any limits, and she challenged all obstacles. Her **compromise** with the environment, civil rights, and women's causes were unavoidable moral duties for her.

After leaving the Miami Herald Newspaper in 1923, she dedicated herself in full to her literary career. Her writing mainly focused on conservation efforts in South Florida, a topic she had vast knowledge of and manifested in her book: **The Everglades: River of Grass**, published in 1947. This book was part of a series focusing on the state of American rivers. It contributed to educating the public about the appreciation for these fragile ecosystems considered marshy lands without any value. The profound message transmitted through her work prevails as it did then. In the 1988 edition, a chapter titled '**Forty more years of crisis**' was added, providing information about the changes suffered by the Everglades and the political maneuvers that hindered the fight to save it. For its fiftieth anniversary, a chapter titled '**Coming Together**' was added to address the beginning of the restoration of the Everglades in South Florida in its attempt to correct an announced catastrophe.

ENVIRONMENTAL PROBLEM

The rapid development of both shores, the growth of the agricultural industry, and the population in the center and south of Florida have triggered an increase in the water demand. Furthermore, the sluice, presses, and canal systems that redirect water to the sea affect the quantity and quality of the water needed to sustain the Everglades' ecosystems. The environmental disaster that Marjory anticipated is, sadly, a reality. The government and environmental organizations have been working for a few years on a restoration project without precedent, estimated to last approximately 20 years, at the cost of $10.9 billion.

Marjory was a relentless visionary in her quest to raise awareness and get the community together under one same interest. She was crucial in founding the prestigious organization Friends of the Everglades. At the same time, Marjory led campaigns to create the Everglades National Park and Biscayne National Park, and the laws that protect them and their wildlife. She educated the population through her speeches which were addressed to the public and the bureaucratic apparatus.

Marjory was a protagonist in her time. She enlisted in the Navy and joined the Red Cross. She was one of the precursors in the fight for women's right to vote. Marjory was involved in creating a milk fund for families with limited resources, and a member of an activist group that defended the civil rights of the African American population of Miami. She was also tireless. At 95 years old, she founded the Marjory Stoneman Douglas Biscayne Nature Center, which still provides free environmental education to students in South Florida. However, among all her achievements, history has consecrated her as the "Grand Dame of the Everglades" and "Grandmother of the Glades," for her dedication to the defense of the environment.

WATER IS LIFE

1.3 million acres of the Everglades wildlife were granted to Marjory Stoneman Douglas as recognition for the fiftieth-anniversary celebration of the National Park. The protected area guarantees the lands won't be sacrificed for future economic developments. She also received the Presidential Medal of Freedom, awarded by former President Bill Clinton in 1993 when Marjory was 103 years old.

MARJORY STONEMAN DOUGLAS'S

MAGICAL CHEST OF WORDS

Sensitivity

Preservation

Precursor

Protagonist

Persistent

Objeclivily

ecosystems

Educate

Demand

Crisis

creativity

Communication

Raise awareness

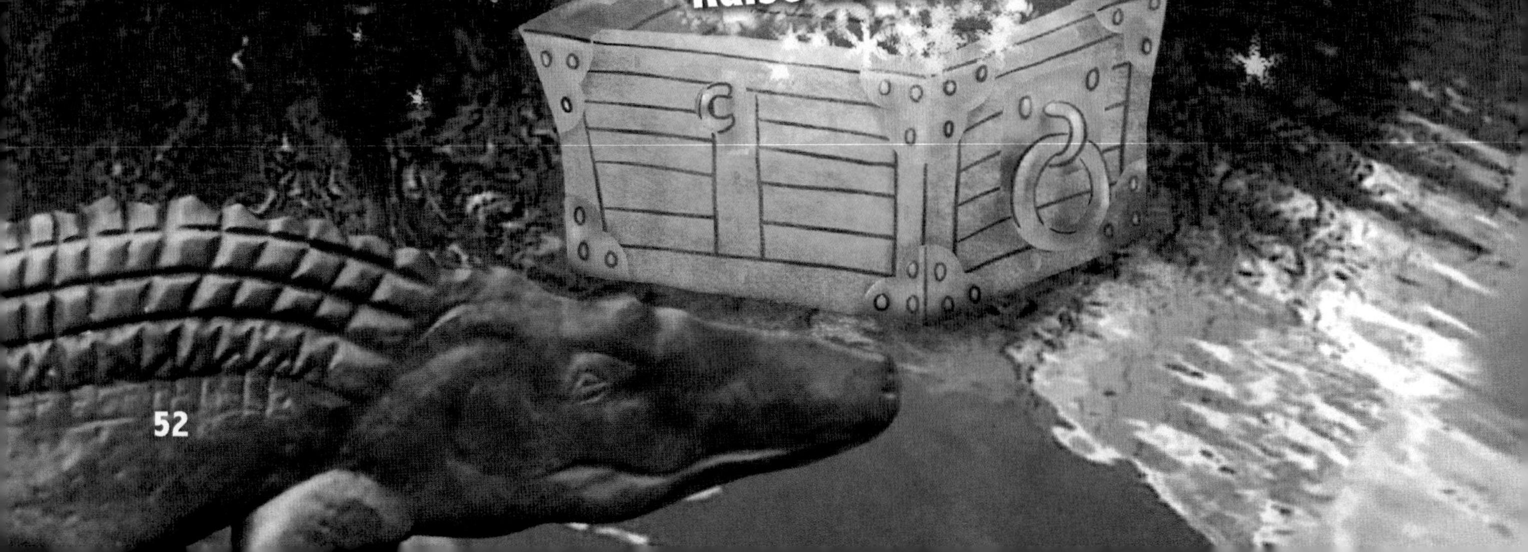

From the chest of words of Marjory Stoneman Douglas, choose the word that corresponds with each definition included in the list below:

- _____: to make people realize something.
- _____: the process of transmitting information between a sender, who gives the message, and a receiver, who receives the message.
- _____: the ability that someone has to create and generate ideas. The creative capacity of an individual. Finding processes, resources, or elements to do something differently or innovatively.
- _____: a sudden change. Complex, bad or difficult situation.
- _____ to ask for or call for something in an authoritative manner.
- _____: specific environments where the vital processes of a community of living beings relate to one another. In a balanced natural ecosystem, animals, plants, and microorganisms interact and share resources, such as water and air, without human intervention.
- _____: to teach, to direct, to address, to instruct.
- _____: impartiality. To present topics or situations independently without any bias.
- _____: perseverant, insistent. To be persistent is to keep trying until achieving something.
- _____: someone who starts something and/or has pioneer ideas (or takes the first steps) about something that will be accepted in the future.
- _____: to take care of, to protect, to guard, or to defend something in anticipation to prevent damage or deterioration.
- _____: the way of thinking and feeling about a particular subject. Sense of perception and intuition, emotiveness.

ACTIVITIES

#32 Read our dreamer's biography, and in each rhombus, write the number of the corresponding sustainable goal mentioned in her life story.

#33 In your notebook, write the answers to the following questions:

1 How did Marjory help in achieving these goals?

2 Through the story, we learned that Marjory advocated for several causes, including civil rights and women's suffrage. Even though her story takes place in the United States, the issues faced by women and ethnic minorities are subjects that affect all of us. How can voting rights contribute to Sustainable Development Goals #5 and #10?

3 What does it mean for you to have the right to choose what you want for your future? How would you feel if someone told you that you have no right to choose?

4 In your notebook, write three reasons why all human beings should have the right to vote and choose the people and the laws that will govern them.

5 What happens when people have this right denied?

"Marjory was the first voice to raise awareness about what we were doing to our quality of life. She was not just a pioneer of the environmental and women's suffrage; she was a prophet, calling out to us to save the environment for our children and our grandchildren."

Lawton Chiles,
Former governor of Florida

Highlight or write on this list all the attributes and characteristics that you consider remarkable about the life and personality of Marjory Stoneman Douglas.

....
....
....
....
....

Use the power of writing to create an impact!

Marjory Stoneman Douglas's book about the Everglades provides valuable information about life there. That is how the Everglades changed from being cataloged as a marsh to being valued as a river.

#35 Select a garden, a park, a riverbank, or your surroundings, and observe the life processes that take place there. Draw and describe them in detail.

....
....
....
....
....
....
....
....
....
....

Elements of COMMUNICATION

I DEFEND LIFE

#37 YOUR LETTER TO: ....

Marjory wrote many letters to influential people who had the power to solve problems, the authority to implement measures, or make recommendations about situations that had to be solved for the community's wellbeing. I invite you to follow that example and exercise your right to freedom of speech. **You, at any age, have the right to express what you feel and what you think.**

Think about a social or ecological problem that affects you or that you consider important. Clearly express that concern and how it affects you and/or other people and possible solutions.

LETTER ADDRESSED TO:

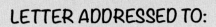

....

Warm greetings.

Problem:
....
....
....

It affects me/us:
....
....
....
....

Possible solutions:
....
....
....

I appreciate your prompt response.

Sincerely,

_____

Your name

ACTIVITY

#38 CREATE YOUR OWN ENVIRONMENTAL EDUCATION CENTER

The Marjory Stoneman Douglas Biscayne Nature Center is part of the 'Grandmother of the Everglades' legacy. Thanks to this center, children and teenagers learn about ecosystems and marine life. They are also encouraged to develop healthy habits to protect the environment.

In *Letters to My Dreams for Planet Earth*, we invite you to create your own Environment Educational Center. To help you, we will give you a list of objectives, and you will complete the rest.

We are sure that you will notice that you have many resources to transform your surroundings into the most wonderful place to research and learn. Don't stay home. Go out, observe and experiment. You will be surprised by all the new ideas that will come to your mind and change your life forever. Let your curiosity take you to unimaginable places!

Objectives	Choose the place, people, or resources
Be in contact with nature.	
Visit places where land animals live.	
Visit places where aquatic animals live.	
Go somewhere you can listen to birds singing and breathe in the scent of flowers.	

Go somewhere you can identify the different types of contamination and understand their process.

Take part in cleaning campaigns at your school, parks, forests, and rivers.

Recycle by separating plastics, paper, glass, and organic residues.

Visit a pesticide-free, organic farm.

Learn about the life of bees and visit an apiary.

Take part in ornamental plants or tree-planting campaigns.

Help to separate trash from recyclable materials.

Write about your experiences and what you have learned about the environment.

Discuss environmental issues, identify their causes, consequences, and come up with ideas about possible solutions.

Continue with your list. There is so much more you can do...

LISTEN TO THE VOICE OF **DR. RAQUEL CHAN**

Argentina, 1959

Thanks to Dr. Raquel Chan, we have a seed more resistant to droughts!

Visionary Dr. Raquel Chan, an Argentine biologist, is one of the most prominent scientists in Latin America. She leads a team of scientists at the Coastal Agrobiotechnology Institute (IAL-UNL-CONICET), sponsored by the National University of the Litoral (UNL) and the National Council on Scientific and Technological Research (CONICET). Her team created the most drought-resistant seed, the HAHB-4.2 gene stemming from sunflowers, which also makes crops more tolerant to the salinity of the soil.

Dr. Chan commented that sunflowers have many genes. By identifying the ones that carry out certain functions within the plant, they were able to isolate the gene responsible for tolerating drought. With this discovery, whether there is a drought or not, the production of soy, wheat, and corn, which are the staple foods of many countries, can be duplicated.

One of Dr. Chan's concerns is the need for food estimated for 2050 when the planet will have 3 billion more people and limited possibilities to increase farming areas. According to experts, we will need to produce 60% more food and crops to meet the population's needs.
What will happen in the year 2070?
How much food will we need to survive?

Dr. Chan defines herself as a very dedicated person who enjoys what she does. She comments that her career is very demanding since scientists face difficulties in their own countries carrying out the experiments and research they want and need to do.

To answer the following questions, think about your surroundings and the possible limitations to carrying out a research project. Share them with your friends, family, and teachers. Analyze the situation, identify and describe obstacles, and suggest solutions

- Which difficulties is Dr. Chan referring to?
- Explain the significance of the discovery by Dr. Chan and her team.
- What would you like to research and why if you were a scientist?
- What are some of the scientific discoveries that have been most beneficial to humankind and planet Earth?
- Which discoveries do you consider have been used against humanity and planet Earth?

Modifying the genetics of our food, is it good... is it wrong or... it depends?

I invite you to research this critical topic and create a table where you can compare the positive and negative aspects. For your analysis, keep in mind the effects of overpopulation, global warming, and the different perspectives about the environmental issues we have studied in this book. To make this research more exciting and participatory, invite other people to talk about the subject and ask them to share possible solution.

You can write your conclusions and publish them on social media or in your school's newspaper.

Remember that we are part of both the problem and the solution.
There's no need to go far looking for a change!
Change begins with oneself!

DR. RAQUEL CHAN'S

MAGICAL CHEST OF WORDS

Agro
Bio
Technology
Agrobiotechnology
Biology
Biotechnology
Biologist
Gene
Genetics
Drought

ACTIVITY

#40 Read our dreamer's biography, and in each rhombus, write the number of the corresponding sustainable goal mentioned in her life story.

ACTIVITY

#41

From the chest of words of Dr. Raquel Chan, choose the word that corresponds with each definition included in the list below:

- _____: related to farming fields.
- _____: Greek root meaning *life*.
- _____: the combination of theories and techniques that allow for the practical use of scientific knowledge. This word also comes from the Greek *tekhné* (art, technique, job) and *logía* (discourse, treaty, or science).
- _____: the use of technology for the genetic manipulation (GM) of seeds to produce new varieties of crops more resistant to droughts, freezing temperatures, plagues, and illnesses. It is also applied to vaccines, identifying genetic maps, and the cloning of farm animals.
- _____: the science that studies life. It comes from the union of two Greek roots: *bio* (life) and *logía* (discourse, treaty, or science).
- _____: the branch of biology that uses live cells in the development of new products or processes through the use of technology. Its wide scope includes the food industry, farming, and medicine.
- _____: a scientist expert in the study and research of all living beings of the planet in all their forms, at the molecular, biochemical, physiological, functional, and environmental levels. A biologist is a researcher with ample knowledge of macroscopic beings, such as animals and plants, and microscopic beings, like bacteria, cells, genes, and viruses.
- _____: a unit of information. In biology, it refers to the DNA (deoxyribonucleic acid) sequence that constitutes the functional unit for transmitting hereditary traits. Its root comes from the Greek *génos*, which means race, lineage, offspring. DNA stores our genetic inheritance.
- _____: the study of genes to understand how biological inheritance is transmitted from generation to generation through DNA. It's one of the major branches of modern biology and includes other subjects like biochemistry and cellular biology.
- _____: the lack of rain that triggers shortages of water for a prolonged period affecting the needs of plants, animals, and humans.

DR. ADRIANA OCAMPO URIA

Colombia, 1955

"The field of science and space is full of exceptional opportunities, but we still need more women to become part of space exploration, which is extraordinary."

Conquering new frontiers in space
Reaching space was her dream. And she did it!

Our visionary Adriana Ocampo Uria was born in Colombia; she carried out her primary studies in Argentina. Later, as a teenager, she moved with her family to California, United States.

Her interest in space exploration was so determinant that she paved the way to reach her goal from a very young age. Not having finished her secondary studies yet, she was already working as a volunteer for the Jet Propulsion Laboratory, a research center specializing in building and operating crewless spaceships for NASA. At first, Adriana was attracted to aerospace engineering. But, later, she discovered that her true passion was the study of planets. Imagine how exciting it must be to work next to many scientists on projects that are unique in their fields: Earth mapping, expeditions to Mars, Jupiter, Pluto, and its five moons, and other projects carried out by NASA.

Adriana Ocampo, who has dedicated her life to studying the solar system and has participated in planning missions to Mars and Jupiter, leads NASA's New Frontiers program. Our visionary's logbook is filled with trips to infinity. In 2016, after a five-year-long interplanetary journey, the space probe Juno –which travels at speeds higher than 16 miles per second and orbits Jupiter vertically– arrived in the planet's vicinity for the first time on a mission that lasted 20 months.

In different media interviews, Adriana has remarked that Jupiter is a puzzling planet. It has days that are 10 hours long; its winds are the fastest in the solar system at speeds of more than 223 miles per hour, and it could be a **protostar** since it emits more energy than it receives from the Sun. The information collected by the space probe Juno reaches Earth, specifically NASA's control center, in a record time of 48 minutes.

According to scientists, this mission to Jupiter will help understand the climate of that planet and will provide knowledge about the formation of the solar system, the planets, and the distribution of the elements. "Learning about this sort of thing can help us understand the mechanisms that could lead us to have a new source of energy, how to use hydrogen, which is present in that planet and so abundant everywhere in the universe."

The scientific work of Adriana Ocampo and her team takes the human experience to the most distant points of infinity, like the journey to Pluto that took eight years. It's the farthest planet that we have been able to reach. Important information about Pluto was sent back to Earth to learn, understand, and prepare ourselves to face the future.

Adriana Ocampo is one of the scientists with the most experience in space exploration worldwide. She is a geology expert at the University of California. She also holds a master's degree in planetary geology science from the California State University, Northridge (CSUN), and a Ph.D. from Vrije Universiteit in Amsterdam. She has been selected by Discover Magazine as one of the 50 most influential women in science. She's currently working on researching impact craters and massive extinctions.

Of course, we can! I invite you to travel to your future:
USE YOUR IMAGINATION.

It's the year 2050, you live in the city of _____, located in
_____. You like that city because _____
_____
_____
_____
_____
_____ Its landscape is _____
_____ and the weather is ____
_____. You work at
_____ as a _____. You are in charge
of _____
_____
_____
_____
_____. Next June 25th you will travel with your family to the city
of _____, located in _____,
at a distance of _____ (hours) (minutes) (seconds). You are
attending a convention about new scientific advancements. Your friend
_____, expert in _____
_____, will present _____
_____
_____. Your girlfriend/boyfriend/partner_____,
expert in _____ will talk about the
importance of _____

_____
_____
_____.
And you will present a project that you have been working on for several years. Thanks to you and the team of _____ that you lead, you have found the solution to _____
_____
_____
Several _____ are interested in supporting your work because _____
_____
_____
_____.
After the conference, you plan to take a few days of rest with your family. For that, you will travel by _____ to go to _____, a place near the convention titled: _____ _____, were they have the latest forms of entertainment: _____
_____
_____
_____
_____
_____
_____.
You are happy because it has been a long time that you haven't enjoyed such an exciting vacation. You relax and think that, for your next vacation you would like to go to _____,
since you have heard that there _____
_____
_____.
But for now, you had better enjoy the present because time flies!

DR. ADRIANA OCAMPO URIA'S

MAGICAL CHEST OF WORDS

Protostar
Interplanetary
Space engineering
Engineering
geology
Energy

ACTIVITY

#43 Read our dreamer's biography, and in each rhombus, write the number of the corresponding sustainable goal mentioned in her life story.

From the chest of words of Dr. Adriana Ocampo Uria, choose the word that corresponds with each definition included in the list below:

- _____: the capacity to carry out a task, to emerge, to transform or to put something into motion. The word comes from the Greek *enérgeia*, which means: activity, operation, a force of action.

- _____: is the natural science that studies the internal and external composition of planet Earth and its evolutionary processes along the geological time (approximately 4,567 million years). It is also applied to the study of the other bodies and matter in the solar system (astrogeology or planetary geology).

- _____: the combination of scientific and empirical knowledge and the application of technology for the optimal conversion of materials and forces of nature for the practical use of humanity through innovation, invention, development, and improvement of techniques and tools. Engineering is also considered art due to the use of human beings' imaginary and creative capacity to conceive and conceptualize things that do not yet exist and transform knowledge into something practical.

- _____: is a branch of engineering that studies spaceships and deals with the design of propelling vehicles and the artifacts that will be placed in outer space.

- _____: refers to the space zone between two or more planets, or beyond space.

- _____: is the evolutionary period of a star, from its beginnings as a molecular cloud composed of hydrogen, helium, and dust particles, until it starts to contract. Protostars with a mass similar to that of the Sun can take 100 million years to evolve from a molecular cloud to a star.

EARTH'S
Bill of Rights

EARTH HAS THE RIGHT TO LIFE. If Earth lives to its fullest, the living systems and the natural processes it holds can survive and regenerate. Earth has the right to its own existence.

EARTH HAS THE RIGHT TO DIVERSITY. All species that inhabit it have the right to their own identity, the preservation of their genetic integrity, vital functions, and respect for their existence and habitat.

EARTH HAS THE RIGHT TO ITS BIOCAPACITY. Ecosystems have the ability to provide useful natural resources and absorb the waste generated by humans to the scale and limit of their own capacity.

EARTH HAS THE RIGHT TO WATER. The life and reproduction of Earth's species and all its elements depend on the functionality of its cycle, quantity, and the quality of this resource, free of contamination.

EARTH HAS THE RIGHT TO CLEAN AIR. The preservation of the air's quality and composition and its protection against contamination are vital to maintaining systms alive.

EARTH HAS THE RIGHT TO HAVE A BALANCE. Its balance depends on maintaining its interrelations, interdependence, complementarity, functionalities, cycles, and the regeneration of its vital processes.

EARTH HAS THE RIGHT TO A LIFE FREE OF CONTAMINATION. Earth and its living systems need to be kept from contamination caused by pollution, toxic waste, and radioactive materials.

EARTH HAS THE RIGHT TO THE RESTORATION OF ITS LIVING SYSTEMS. Human activity affects living systems directly or indirectly; therefore, Earth has the right to have actions undertaken to neutralize, correct, and recover its vital processes.

EARTH HAS THE RIGHT TO RESPECT ITS OWN RIGHTS. We all are THE EARTH. We all have the same rights.

I'm
MY
PLANET

"...At the current rate of deforestation, all of the tropical rainforests will be gone partway through the next century. If we allow this destruction to happen, the world will lose the richest storehouse of genetic information on the planet. And along with it possible cures for many of the diseases that afflict us. Indeed, hundreds of important medicines now in common use are derived from plants and animals of the tropical rainforests".

Earth in the Balance: Forging a New Common Purpose
Al Gore, former US Vice President
2007 Nobel Peace Prize

ACTIVITY **#45** Get inspired!

a. Think about that citation and rewrite it using positive language.

b. Select one or several Earth's rights and write a poem or short story.

PLANET EARTH'S
Magical Chest of Words

Contamination

Biocapacity

Balance of the planet

Interdependencies

Interrelations

Hábitat

Complementarity

Biodiversity

Cycles

Diversity

Regeneration

Life

- _____: the word has a Latin origin: *vita*, which in turn comes from the Greek *bios*, meaning life. From biology: life can be born, grow, reproduce, and die.

- _____: refers to the abundance of different things and the difference in variety in everything that exists.

- _____: or biological diversity, is the combination of living beings (animals, plants, organisms, and terrestrial and marine ecosystems), their environment, and the relationship between different species that inhabit the planet after millions of years of evolution.

- _____: it's the place that, with its characteristics, allows for the existence of a specific group of living beings, guaranteeing their cycle to be born, grow, reproduce, and die. A habitat could be a lake, a marsh, a glacier, a bush, etc. Human beings also need their habitat.

- _____: the capacity that a biologically productive area has to regenerate renewable resources and absorb the environmental waste produced by human consumption. When the impact of consumption is higher than the capacity of that area to renew its natural resources, we are breaking sustainability and the balance of planet Earth.

- _____: refers to the presence of elements and substances that negatively affect the environment because they trigger damages and alterations that endanger ecosystems. There are different types of contamination: water, soil, air, and the contamination of visual and acoustic surroundings.

- _____: refers to **sustainability**. The exploitation rate of natural resources cannot be higher than Earth's ability to renew itself and replace its own resources. Also, we must generate minimal amounts of residue so that the planet can naturally absorb them and for our environmental impact not to break the chain of life.

- _____: refer to mutual relationships among people, objects, and other elements. Human beings and the environment have an interrelation. Whatever one does, affects the other.

- _____: are relations based on dependency, responsibility, and a group of factors and principles where several parties (people, countries, and living beings in general) establish agreements and undertake actions in a way that all those involved can benefit. It's a chain of cooperation where dependence is reciprocal and equitable.

- _____: comes from the Latin word *cyclus* and the Greek *kyklus*, which means circle or wheel. It's a period where different events or processes occur. Once it's finished, it repeats in the same order, such as the cycle of life, water, rocks, etc.

- _____: is a reciprocal relationship of integration between parties. The quality of being complimentary means to perfect or complete another thing or party.

- _____: it's mechanism of restoration or recovery of living beings to rehabilitate or to re-establish themselves. In human beings, we can see this mechanism in our nails, hair, skin, bones, and liver. Every species is different.

I AM: _____
MY HABITAT IS: _____

I AM: _____
MY HABITAT IS: _____

Thinkers' Roundtable

#47

- What waste or residue do we humans produce?

     Analyze your environment and determine the possible contaminants where you live or study. Can you do something to make it better?

     Look for the meaning of ecological footprint. Try to describe it in terms of a person, a city, a country, and the world.

- Can we minimize our ecological footprint? How?

- Why is it important to protect biodiversity?

Research who was "Lonesome George" and write his story.

#48

Activity:
Hello dreamer, we invite you to research our names and our habitat.

I AM: _____
MY HABITAT IS: _____

I AM: _____
MY HABITAT IS: _____

I AM: _____
MY HABITAT IS: _____

EARTH'S RIGHTS

#48

We're going to help you with a few simple steps:

The experts who designed the Master Plan for the 17 Sustainable Development Goals would like your group of thinkers to read about Earth's Rights and verify which are protected by the 17 goals.

Goal: _____

Earth's Rights: _____

_____

_____

_____

_____

_____

_____

The team of experts would like you to answer the following questions:

1. Are all Earth's Rights included in the 17 Sustainable Development Goals?

_____

_____

_____

_____

_____

2. If you could add other goals to the 17 Sustainable Goals to protect Earth's Rights, which would you add? Why?

_____

_____

_____

_____

_____

_____

_____

#49

Visionaries in action for
PLANET EARTH

Complete this table and start a plan of action today

Problem or need	Describe the problem or need	Describe the actions you are going to take	What do you need for this action?	How are you going to measure the results?
Garbage				
Plastics				
Water				
Information				
Sensitivity				
Caring for animals				
Planting trees				
Contamination				
Energy conservation				
Consumption				
Change				

#50

Write in your notebook: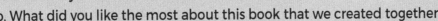

a. What did you learn from each of our visionaries?

b. What did you like the most about this book that we created together?

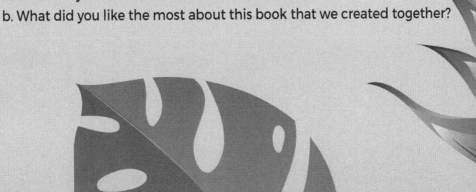

DEAR VISIONARY:

OUR JOURNEY DOES NOT STOP HERE.
THIS IS JUST THE BEGINNING.

#51

You have already learned that it is vital visionary have dreams, and you must fight to make them a reality. Now you have the power of knowledge and life examples so you can inspire others to make changes too.

INVITE PEOPLE TO WRITE DOWN WHAT THEIR DREAMS ARE ALL ABOUT ON THESE PAGES.
DREAMS ARE A CHAIN... AND MANY WILL REACH THEIR DREAMS, THANKS TO THE GREATNESS OF YOURS.

Place your picture
HERE

PEGA

I'm
_____
Write your name

I Have a Dream for Planet Earth

I HAVE A DREAM

 Let's think and embrace the positive affirmations inspired by our dreamers

2 Let your heart speak!
Write comments in your diary about each of these affirmations.
Recognize your greatness!

because:
....
....
....

Inspired by
Your dream

I'm VISIONARY

because:
....
....
....

Inspired by
Dr. Adriana Ocampo Uria

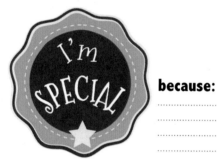

because:
....
....
....

Inspired by
Your dream

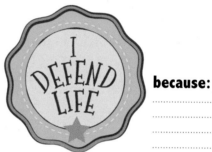

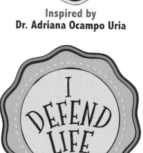

I DEFEND LIFE

because:
....
....
....
....

Inspired by
Marjory Stoneman Douglas

because:
....
....
....

Inspired by
Boyan Slat

I'm CLEVER

because:
....
....
....

Inspired by
Dr. Raquel Chan

because:
....
....
....
....

Inspired by
My planet Earth

3 ¡Remember this Always!

82

CALENDAR OF THE EARTH

Activity:
Write the dates in the yellow circles and complete the calendar.

JANUARY

WORLD ENVIRONMENTAL EDUCATION DAY

WORLD REDUCTION OF CO_2 DAY

FEBRUARY

WORLD WETLANDS DAY

MARCH

WORLD NATURE DAY

WORLD WATER DAY

APRIL

WORLD EARTH DAY

MAY

INTERNATIONAL RECYCLING DAY

INTERNATIONAL DAY FOR BIOLOGICAL DIVERSITY

JUNE

WORLD ENVIRONMENT DAY

WORLD OCEANS DAY

JULY

INTERNATIONAL PLASTIC BAG FREE DAY

AUGUST

INTERNATIONAL DAY AGAINST NUCLEAR TESTS

SEPTEMBER

INTERNATIONAL DAY FOR THE PRESERVATION OF THE OZONE LAYER

OCTOBER

WORLD ANIMAL DAY

WORLD HABITAT DAY

INTERNATIONAL DAY FOR NATURAL DISASTER REDUCTION

NOVEMBER

INTERNATIONAL DAY FOR PREVENTING THE EXPLOITATION OF THE ENVIRONMENT IN WAR AND ARMED CONFLICTS

DECEMBER

WORLD SOIL DAY

Made in United States
Orlando, FL
15 April 2022

16841603R00049